Original title:
Jasmine Journeys

Copyright © 2025 Creative Arts Management OÜ
All rights reserved.

Author: Victor Mercer
ISBN HARDBACK: 978-1-80566-724-7
ISBN PAPERBACK: 978-1-80566-853-4

A Voyage through Green

In the garden where weeds do play,
The gnomes trip over, led astray.
Rabbits laugh, with carrots in tow,
While ants host dances, quite the show.

I found a snail who claims to race,
But irony begs him to slow his pace.
The daisies giggle as butterflies swoop,
While I trip over my own shoelace loop.

Scented Stories Unfold

Flowers gossip in the breeze's ear,
Bees drop puns, just to endear.
In puddles of sunlight, frogs sing jokes,
As cheeky sparrows share wild pokes.

Petunias often roll their eyes,
At daisies telling tall, tall lies.
But who can blame them, we all know,
That plants have secrets, shy to show.

The Allure of Nature's Touch

In the meadow, clovers make a fuss,
Bouncing about, no time to discuss.
A lazy squirrel, on a branch, naps,
While chipmunks plan, with tiny maps.

Old oak trees chuckle, they're wise and spry,
Whispering tales as leaves wave goodbye.
But watch out, my friend, the kite may steal,
An afternoon toast of wind-tinged meal.

Secrets of the Garden Path

Down the lane where shadows dwell,
Worms share secrets, fond of a shell.
The roses barter for a wit or two,
While tangy vines make sure to boo.

Tread lightly on the bustling ground,
For giggles hide in every mound.
The sun nods, it's a comical plight,
In a world where plants know how to bite!

Petals in the Breath of Time

In a garden where laughter blooms,
Petals twirl like dancers in costumes.
The clock ticks backward, is that a prank?
I'm lost in the giggles, a floral sank.

Bumblebees buzz with a comic tone,
Mistaking the sun for their comfy home.
The roses burst out in fits of glee,
As I chase a butterfly, wild and free.

The Hidden Garden Path

A path through mischief, tall weeds so sly,
Draws me closer, oh my, oh my!
Each step I take, a twig snaps loud,
The squirrels above snicker, feeling proud.

A garden gnome grins with a cheeky smirk,
In the wild undergrowth, the shadows lurk.
A sign says 'Beware of the weeds that dance',
But oh, what fun! Let's give it a chance!

Whispers Carried by the Breeze

The breeze carries secrets from flowers' lips,
Tickling my ears, just like goofy quips.
"Hey there, buddy, don't step on my toes!"
Said a daisy to thistle, as the laughter grows.

Crisp leaves crackle in a playful race,
Chasing each other with a sprightly grace.
A gust bursts forth, sending petals astray,
"Catch me if you can!" they giggle away.

In the Shade of the Sweet-Scented

Underneath blooms, a picnic was laid,
With pastries and jokes, and a sunflower brigade.
They offered me snacks that tickled my nose,
But hey, what's that? A ticklish rose?

Sipping on sweet tea, butterflies tease,
Playing hide and seek through the humming trees.
Laughter erupts, a melodious spree,
In this silly garden, just you and me.

The Language of Petals

In gardens where giggles bloom,
Petals whisper secrets of room.
A flower said, "Rain, not in jest,
I prefer parties; I'm dressed my best!"

Bees wear tuxedos, buzzing loud,
While ants form a conga line proud.
The daisies dance, a sight to see,
They trip over roots—oh dear me!

Through Fields of Delight

In fields of glee, the daisies play,
Chasing butterflies on a sunny day.
"A garden's the place to be hasty!"
Said a petunia, "Just ask my matey!"

With butterflies molding shapes so grand,
They form a parade of colors so planned.
"I'm the best dancer!" shouted the rose,
As petunias wore sunglasses, striking a pose.

Dreams in Full Bloom

In dreams where petals sprout delight,
A dandelion snickered at night.
"I'm not a weed, I'm a wish, can't you see?
I'd rather float far—and be free!"

Lilies giggled at shadows so still,
In moonlit laughs, they dance at will.
"Oh dear! Watch for bees!" they'd chirp in fright,
"But if they sting, we'll just take flight!

Flourishing Footprints

With clumsy roots, we stomp around,
In muddy puddles, joy is found.
"Oops! I slipped, what a slide!"
Giggled the violet, with petals wide.

Across the garden, laughter flies,
As tulips wear hats; oh, what a guise!
"Who wore it better?" they debated in cheer,
Until the wind blew them—oh dear!

Blooms Beneath the Sun

Petals giggle in the breeze,
Swaying softly with the trees.
Bees with hats and little shoes,
Dance around while sipping juice.

Sunlight cascades in a play,
Buds are bouncing, come what may.
A daisy stops, takes a bow,
Waves to all—here's looking now!

Laughing lilies in a row,
Trade their tales of how to grow.
Funny how they twist and twine,
Chasing shadows, feeling fine.

A flower sneezes, "Achoo!"
Spilling pollen, oh, what a to-do!
Nature cracks a silly grin,
Beneath the sun, the fun begins!

Nature's Hidden Paths

In a garden where weeds play tricks,
Pathways form with little flicks.
A squirrel quizzes flowers fair,
"Who's got the best root to share?"

Frogs in shades lounge on a log,
Chasing dreams like a friendly dog.
Hidden paths where mushrooms hum,
Singing tales of whence they come.

Charming critters form a band,
Playing tunes across the land.
A snail drummer, steady and slow,
Keeps the beat while flowers glow.

Laughter bubbles through the soil,
As secrets dance and leaves uncoil.
Nature's paths are full of quirks,
Who knew gardening had such perks?

A Canvas of Blossoms

Colors splash, a painting bold,
Upon the canvas, stories told.
A clownish tulip, wide and bright,
Tickles bees with sheer delight.

Splattered hues—a riotous scene,
With daisies laughing in between.
Petunias wear their finest hats,
While butterflies sway, chatting with bats.

Each bloom strikes a pose, so proud,
Waiting for applause from the crowd.
"Encore!" they shout from all around,
As petals spin and whirl around.

Artists in the garden sway,
Creating magic every day.
On this canvas, humor reigns,
In every leaf, laughter remains!

The Poetry of Botanical Pursuits

Verses sprout in the morning light,
Astronaut herbs reach dizzy height.
Roses pen sonnets, sweet and bold,
With every petal, a story unfolds.

Cacti rhyme with prickly cheer,
While violets snicker—"We're still here!"
In the plots where daisies tease,
Nature's laughter rides the breeze.

A lead actor, a sunflower grand,
Steals the show across the land.
With roots in deep, they take their turn,
Nature persists in this grand yearn.

Fun abounds, each stalk a quill,
Pens that scratch with playful thrill.
In this green poem, joy's the theme,
Botanical wonders reign supreme!

A Symphony of Colors in Bloom.

In the garden, colors collide,
Petals pirouette, gloriously wide.
Bees wear tiny hats, quite absurd,
While butterflies serenade with a word.

A blue jay in socks hops on a twig,
While blooms hold a dance-off, oh so big!
Roses do the cha-cha, tulips the twist,
Nature's party, not to be missed!

Blossoms in the Breeze

Beneath a sky of cotton candy skies,
Flowers gossip, sharing their lies.
Daisies poke fun at the shy old fern,
While dandelions plot their wild return.

A sunflower chuckles with pollen all over,
Honking geese waddle like they're in a rover.
Petunias wear sunglasses, looking so cool,
Nature's rascals, breaking all rules!

A Pathway of Petals

On a path lined with petals, a sight to behold,
Floral footprints giggle, secrets to unfold.
Lilies hike in boots, tulips with flair,
Carnations are plotting to braid their hair.

Wandering weeds with a mischievous grin,
Start a game, 'Who can spin the best spin?'
With every step, laughter follows the trail,
In this petal parade, inevitability prevails!

Whispers of Fragrant Travels

In a world where scents roam free and wild,
Choco-mint roses tease like a playful child.
Lavender laughs with a tickling breeze,
While ginger blooms snack on sweet honeydews.

Camellias scheme with a cheeky plan,
Sending up fragrances like no one can.
The air's an orchestra, laughter a tune,
In this comedic garden, bliss must be strewn!

The Secrets of Blooming Paths

In a garden where flowers sneak,
Petals laugh as the bees all speak.
A hidden path, so bright and bold,
Where secrets of nature's fun unfold.

The daisies dance in sunlit glee,
With tulips plotting a grand spree.
The roses giggle, their thorns misplaced,
As they race, all their beauty embraced.

A squirrel juggles acorns with flair,
While butterflies prance without a care.
The zany vines twist in delight,
A hidden adventure, day or night.

So skip along this blooming lane,
Where laughter echoes, never plain.
With every step, a chuckle found,
In nature's realm, joy abounds!

A Whiff of Adventure

A snip of mint, a dash of sage,
The spices blend like a laughing page.
Each herb whispers tales of yore,
As I sniff and giggle, wanting more.

Cilantro twirls with a cheeky grin,
While rosemary's antics make me spin.
A marjoram mishap, oh what a scene,
All the herbs join this joke routine.

In pots of mischief, they do reside,
Their funny quirks, I cannot hide.
As I wander through this fragrant play,
Every whiff turns the mundane gay.

So take a whiff, join in the fun,
These herbs won't stop till the day is done.
With laughter sprouting from every leaf,
Adventure awaits, beyond belief!

Traversing the Garden's Gifts

With a spade in hand, I venture out,
To find what nature is all about.
A twist of luck in every dig,
Planting humor, maybe a fig?

The carrots chuckle beneath the earth,
While radishes boast of their worth.
A pumpkin grins, round and plump,
In this garden, they all jump!

Tomatoes blushing, ripe and red,
Spinach cracks jokes from its leafy bed.
Zucchini zips by in a flash,
Creating a garden full of sass!

So wander through this jolly patch,
Where every veg has its quirky match.
With laughter growing alongside the seeds,
The garden's gifts fulfill our needs!

The Call of the Blossoming Trail

A trail of petals invites the brave,
Where flowers giggle, and they misbehave.
A call from blooms, oh what a sound,
In this playful path, joy is found.

The daisies wink, the violets tease,
While bumblebees float in the breeze.
Every step brings a new surprise,
In this vibrant realm, laughter flies.

Butterflies flutter with cheeky flair,
A tangle of wings, giggles in the air.
The wildflowers join the raucous show,
In this blossoming path, fun will grow.

So heed the call and laugh along,
Where every petal sings a song.
On this trail of humor and cheer,
Nature's laughter draws us near!

Echoes of Nature's Embrace

In a garden full of giggles,
The flowers dance, oh what a tease.
Bees wear tiny striped wiggles,
Buzzing tunes that aim to please.

Rabbits hop with silly flair,
Chasing shadows, quick and bright.
Squirrels play, without a care,
Through the day and into night.

I tripped on grass, fell on my face,
Laughed out loud with a silly squeal.
The earth spun like a wild race,
Nature's whims, a funny reel.

With every step, a joke unfolds,
Caterpillars sport wisecrack grins.
In this world, laughter beholds,
Nature's pranks where joy begins.

Wandering Among the Fragrant Shadows

Through fragrant paths, I skip and sway,
Dancing shadows tease my feet.
Lemonade sun in bright array,
Makes every moment taste so sweet.

Oh look, a flower with a hat!
Waving petals, a funny sight.
A butterfly made me go splat,
In a bloom, I found delight.

Crickets chirp a funny beat,
While frogs jump in a grand parade.
Nature's rhythm, soft and sweet,
In this chorus, I can't evade.

As I prance and swirl around,
A squirrel sneaks my snack away.
Yet, in laughter I am crowned,
For in humor, I choose to stay.

The Enchanted Pathway

On an enchanted road I roam,
With flowers wearing smiles so wide.
Every bend feels like a home,
Where giggles and bright scent collide.

A cheeky gnome peeked from a bush,
Said, "Mind the bees, they like to buzz!"
I jumped back with a silly hush,
Then laughed, "It's just a little fuzz!"

Twinkle-toed, the fairies prance,
Sprinkling laughter like morning dew.
Every leaf joins in the dance,
Nature's comedy, fresh and new.

I found a frog that thought it cool,
To serenade the hovering flies.
He croaked a tune as I played fool,
In this realm, the heart always flies.

Serenading the Night Blossoms

Under stars, I sing to blooms,
With moonlight twinkling, all aglow.
The night is full of gentle hums,
As laughter fills the air below.

A raccoon donned a fancy coat,
Danced with shadows, what a guy!
Joined by fireflies that emote,
In this midnight high-society.

The petals giggle in the breeze,
As I whisper silly dreams aloud.
Entwined with fragrance, sweet degrees,
In this world, I feel so proud.

With each note, the night expands,
As blossoms sway with gentle grace.
Nature joins in, lending hands,
In this funny, fragrant space.

Echoes of Nature's Song

In the garden, bees take flight,
Buzzing tunes from morn till night.
Worms do the wiggly dance,
While flowers giggle, given the chance.

Squirrels plot a nutty scheme,
Swinging high, they quite esteem.
Butterflies flaunt their lively hues,
While ants march on, with tipsy shoes.

The sun peeks in, the clouds do chase,
Nature's laughter fills the place.
With every rustle, a ticklish tease,
As critters play and dance with ease.

The Fragrance of Memories

Old socks piled in the hall,
Smelling like a fun free-for-all.
Forgotten lunch from yesterday,
Still clinging on in a curious way.

Candles lit with colors bright,
Peeking out from their plastic light.
Mom's potpourri goes on a trip,
While Dad's cologne takes a mighty whip.

Oh, the scents that float and dance,
Each a memory, a silly romance.
A whiff of cake, a dash of pie,
Together they twirl, oh me, oh my!

Wanderlust in Bloom

A pizza box sailed in the breeze,
Chased by hungry, giggling bees.
Frogs on bikes, a hopping race,
Wearing helmets with silly grace.

Clouds roll like cotton candy fluff,
While trees dress up in nature's stuff.
The road is long with twists and turns,
In every corner, the adventure burns.

With toes in mud and shoes askew,
The world is bright, the skies are blue.
Let's ride the rainbows, splash and zoom,
In this wild playground, we surely bloom!

Trails of Enchantment

Through the woods, a giggle slips,
Where pixies dance and the rabbit flips.
Fern hats on, they prance around,
With squeaky voices that astound.

Mushrooms wear polka dot shoes,
While grumpy owls just snooze and snooze.
Dancing shadows, whispering trees,
Swirling tales ride on the breeze.

A raccoon waves with a cheeky grin,
While a sly fox invites us in.
On trails of wonder, we take our flight,
In this enchanted world of delight.

Odyssey of the Night Flower

In the garden, I lost my shoe,
The flower said, 'You smell like dew!'
With petals dancing all around,
I tripped on roots, fell to the ground.

The moonlight chuckled at my plight,
As crickets played a tune of night.
A bumblebee buzzed in my ear,
'Get up quick, the dance floor's near!'

I joined the blooms in their parade,
While laughing at the mess I'd made.
The daisies pinched me on the side,
A flower brawl I couldn't hide!

So if you stroll where night blooms thrive,
Be cautious, friends, and stay alive!
For petals may lead you astray,
In laughter's wild and floral play.

Blossoms and the Heart's Whisper

A sunflower winked, it stole my heart,
In a game of tag, we'd surely part.
Roses blushed, they knew my game,
While violets snickered, feeling the same.

The tulips teased with a sway and sway,
'Come join our dance, what do you say?'
But tripping on roots, I clutch my side,
And simply giggled as I took a ride.

A bumblebee buzzed, what a strange gig,
Said, 'Life's a bloom, go on, do a jig!'
We twirled through petals, laughter rang,
As flowers chirped and the night sang.

So if you find a heart so free,
Know it's just a flower's decree!
For in this garden, love takes flight,
With giggles echoing in the night.

Treading through Floral Fantasies

In a patch of daisies, I saw a hat,
Worn by a squirrel who looked quite fat!
He tipped it low, with flair galore,
'This garden's mine, who wants some more?'

The poppies giggled, rolling with glee,
While I just stared, what could this be?
With petals waving, calling my name,
I joined his parade, oh, what a game!

The roses swayed, a royal court,
Joined us quick for a floral sport.
We twirled and danced, oh what a flap,
With flowers laughing, I took a nap!

So tread softly on nature's heart,
For in these blooms, you play a part.
In fanciful gardens where laughter's spun,
Just keep your hat on, it's all in fun!

A Field of Moonlit Mysteries

In a field of blooms, surprise unfurled,
A daisy claimed, 'I rule this world!'
With petals high, it strutted about,
I giggled hard, what a fuss, no doubt!

The night was bright with twinkling lights,
While flowers whispered of wild delights.
But when I joined their moonlit play,
We spun around till the break of day!

A gathering of petals laughed in jest,
'Take heed, dear friend, this is a test!'
I stumbled forward, plucking a sprout,
And found my way in, the fun was out!

So tread lightly where blossoms bloom,
For laughter hides in each sweet room.
In this field of wild histories,
You'll find the joys of mysteries.

Scented Footsteps of Dawn

In the morning glow, I stride,
With petals stuck on my side.
Birds laugh as I trip and sway,
Oh, what a start to this fine day!

Sneaky bees buzz all around,
They dance like clowns without a sound.
I slip on dew, it's quite a show,
While flowers giggle, 'Look at her go!'

A quick shift to the tulip patch,
Where ants make plans, a sneaky batch.
They scheme a party, I can't resist,
But can't they see? I'm on the list!

With each fold of my crumpled hat,
I wonder if it's too much or not.
The morning laughs, it can't be wrong,
Adventures start when chaos is strong!

A Voyage Through Garden Secrets

There's treasure here beneath the vines,
A hidden gem that always shines.
A carrot says, 'I'm quite the catch!'
But then trips on a cabbage patch!

The daisies gossip in a row,
While I just seek the garden's glow.
I sail on weeds, like ships at sea,
Hoping to find the world's best tea!

A rogue tomato threw a fit,
'Why can't they see I'm full of wit?'
I laugh so hard, my sides do ache,
While exploring this whimsical lake.

And when I drop my hat in mud,
The lilies squeal, they make a thud.
The garden's charm, a playful jest,
In this wild voyage, I am blessed!

The Dance of Delicate Strands

In windswept fields, the grasses twirl,
A curious snail makes quite a swirl.
He spins and slips, a tiny star,
His friends all cheer, 'You've come so far!'

Petals fall like confetti bright,
As bugs throw parties in pure delight.
With a hiccup and a sly little grin,
They toast to victory, let the fun begin!

A dandelion shouts, 'Here, here!'
All my worries vanish, I have no fear.
On delicate strands, we laugh and prance,
Under the sun, we all take a chance.

But oh, the breeze plays tricks on me,
It lifts my hat like a wild spree.
With each gust, the garden spins,
In this dancing chaos, everyone wins!

Blooms Beneath Starlit Canopies

At night the blooms begin to hum,
And bugs invite all friends to come.
With tiny lights and laughter loud,
The garden party draws a crowd.

Beneath the stars, we kick up dust,
A firefly's glow is quite a must.
The moon winks down, a playful sight,
As daisies wiggle, what a night!

We trade our stories, tales of woe,
Of sneaky squirrels and water's flow.
While crickets chirp a soothing tune,
I swear I caught one dancing too!

So here's to blooms, both bold and shy,
With petals waving as they fly.
Under this canopy, carousing free,
In these nighttime laughs, I'll always be!

Trails of Aromatic Tales

In gardens where giggles grow,
The plants gossip soft and low.
A rose rolled by, fell on its face,
Said, "This dirt is my happy place!"

Butterflies dance on a breeze,
Tickling petals with such ease.
A daisy tripped, fell on a bee,
Squeaked, "Watch it! You're stinging me!"

The sunflowers wear hats so wide,
They bask in rays, filled with pride.
They gossip about the moon's light,
"She can't dance, but oh! What a sight!"

Lavender laughs, wit so spry,
With thyme and basil, they drift by.
They swap recipes right in the sun,
"And who said herbs can't have fun?"

The Secret Language of Flowers

In whispers soft, blooms start to chat,
A tulip brought a curious cat.
"What's your secret?" asked with a grin,
"How do you bloom? Where do you begin?"

The daisies winked, oh what a tease,
"We tickle the sun; it's a breezy freeze!"
Lilies laughed, "Join in our game,
But don't get stuck, or feel the shame!"

Hydrangeas shouted in colors bold,
"Pick me up! I'm a sight to behold!"
But roses sighed, with a shake of their heads,
"I'm too prickly, stick to flowerbeds."

Their gossip spread through the garden fair,
With petals spinning in fragrant air.
The bees took note, buzzed with delight,
"We'll keep your secrets, oh what a sight!"

Blooming in Every Season

From winter's cold to summer's burn,
Blooms have antics that make you turn.
The snowdrop shimmies in the frost,
"Look at me, I'm the one not lost!"

Spring brings tulips dressed in jests,
Frolicking fiercely, they do their best.
While pansies chat with a cheeky grin,
"Life's a party, come join in!"

As summer sun makes petals sway,
Sunflowers join in, shout hooray!
With every breeze, they sway and dance,
In floral fashion, they take a chance.

Then autumn rolls in with colors bright,
The leaves join flowers for one last flight.
"Let's scatter seeds!" the garden roars,
And bloom once more, outside your doors!

A Stroll Through Scented Memories

Take a stroll through memory's lane,
Where scents of laughter dance like rain.
A whiff of mint, a dash of thyme,
Remember that cake? Oh, what a crime!

Petunias recall a picnicking crew,
Who spilled their juice—what a hue!
With bees buzzing tales of sweet delight,
They chuckle under the stars each night.

Roses whisper of love that's sweet,
With every sigh, they tap their feet.
Dandelions giggle, blowing their fluff,
"Life's too short, let's play rough!"

Old blooms gather under the moon's gaze,
Sharing stories from yesterdays.
In petals soft, memories unfold,
In a fragrant world, let laughter bold!

The Essence of Adventure

In a land where flowers play,
A bee tried to dance, but fell all day.
With petals in a dizzy swirl,
He went for nectar, not for a twirl.

A squirrel donned a tiny hat,
Claiming he could outsmart a cat.
Chasing shadows, he lost his way,
And found himself stuck in a bouquet.

A snail raced fast, or so he'd boast,
But a leaf blocked him, that's no joke—
He built a castle made of grime,
Felt like a king, just wasting time!

So here we laugh, as quests unfold,
In gardens where stories constantly told.
With silly critters leading the cheer,
Adventure awaits with a wink and a sneer.

Gardens of the Mind

In the depths of my thoughts, flowers bloom bright,
A garden of giggles, what a strange sight!
Twirling flamingos on a wobbly line,
Making lemonade with whimsy and lime.

Thoughts drift like petals on a soft breeze,
A peacock in pajamas, oh please!
He struts around with a flair like no other,
Stealing snacks from his hairy old brother.

In this mindscape, a rabbit in heels,
Tells stories of donuts and curious meals.
He hops on the clouds, just living his dream,
In the land of the giggles, nothing's as it seems.

So let's take a stroll through this whimsical place,
Where laughter grows wild, at its very own pace.
With every petal, a story to find,
In the colorful blanket of a curious mind.

Blossoms Beneath the Stars

Under twinkling lights, a bloom made a wish,
To dance with the moon, oh what a delight!
But slipped on the dew, went 'whoops' with a swish,
And landed on grass, what a silly sight!

A raccoon in shades, thought he was the one,
To host a grand party, full of fun under sun.
But as he was cracking a nut on the tree,
He fell on the cake, oh dear, what a spree!

Stars giggled softly, as they witnessed the show,
With petals twirling high, a whimsical glow.
Fireflies danced as they lit up the scene,
In this nighttime garden, where laughter's routine.

So let's toast to the blooms that sway in night's air,
With friends stumbling joyfully, without a care.
In the garden of stars, where memories are made,
Every blossom reflects a funny escapade.

Petal-Paved Roads

Along the path where petals are strewn,
A frog wearing glasses croaked a fine tune.
He conducted the traffic of ants on a spree,
As they marched to a beat, all silly and free.

A butterfly wore a tutu, quite bright,
Twisted and twirled in a fluttering flight.
But tripped on a daisy and landed face-first,
In puddles of laughter, what joy was dispersed!

The sun played peekaboo with clouds up high,
While a snail made a smoothie, just wondering why.
Everyone gathered for a sip and a cheer,
As the petal-paved roads brought together a sphere.

So let's skip down this giggly lane,
With creatures of whimsy, where laughter's a train.
Onwards we march, through this forest of fun,
In a world paved with petals, where joy's never done.

Whispers of the Moonlit Bloom

In the garden where laughter grows,
A flower once slipped on its toes.
With petals a-sway and a dance so spry,
It tangled its roots, oh my, oh my!

Who knew blooms could bust a move?
A conga line that makes you groove.
With leaves all a-flutter, they prance about,
Swaying to a rhythm, no doubt, no doubt!

One blossom thought it could sing a tune,
But tripped on a daffodil under the moon.
A chorus of giggles from stalks around,
As pollen was scattered, oh what a sound!

So if you dare glide in petals' embrace,
Watch out for the blooms that want to race.
For in the night's silliness, laughter can bloom,
And a dance with the flowers fills up every room!

The Path of Fragrant Dreams

Amidst the hedges where scents collide,
A bumblebee rode on the catnip slide.
With goggles on tight and a tiny hat,
It buzzed up the lane like a furry acrobat.

A sunflower called, "Come play with me!"
"I'm busy!" said mint, "Can't you see?"
But petals tossed in a playful breeze,
Enticed them all to join with ease.

The lilacs chuckled as the rose took flight,
Doing loop-de-loops in the soft moonlight.
While daisies blushed at the sight of the show,
And laughed 'til their roots felt a ticklish glow.

On fragrant pathways, dreams take a spin,
With giggles and wiggles—let's all dive in!
For in every bloom where laughter is sown,
The sweetest of paths are never alone!

Blossoms Under Twilight Skies

Under twilight skies where petals sway,
A dandelion wished it could dance and play.
With dreams of a limbo, it bent so low,
Just to impress every passerby so slow.

The tulips laughed, their colors ablaze,
With stories of worms and their silly ways.
They formed a parade, all in a row,
As the daisies cheered, yelling, "Here we go!"

A clump of wild roses, so bold and bright,
Tried to spin circles, oh what a sight!
They twirled and they stumbled, a comical mess,
Rolling down hills in frothy excess.

So when day fades, and night softly sighs,
Join in the fun beneath dreamy skies.
For blossoms in laughter bring joy all around,
In petals of humor, pure bliss can be found!

Petals on the Wind

A gust of wind swept through the grove,
Chasing petals that started to rove.
With giggles and tickles, they zoomed and swirled,
Creating a chaos that spun and twirled.

One petal flew high, then landed with flair,
Right on the nose of a bunny, quite rare.
The bunny just chuckled, gave it a shake,
And tossed the poor petal into the lake.

The roses were jealous, "We want a ride!"
They plotted and planned with petals wide.
But the wind just laughed, it was not their friend,
As they watched the adventures, around the bend.

So if you find petals dancing on air,
Remember their journeys, so light and so rare.
For in every flap, flutter, and spin,
Lies a story of fun, let the laughter begin!

Flora's Hidden Tales

In the garden, plants conspire,
Whispers of leaves, they retire.
A sunflower wears shades of glee,
While daisies gossip, who'd disagree?

A rose tried dancing, slipped on dew,
The tulips giggled, 'What a view!'
Bees buzz by with much ado,
'Look at that rose, she's lost her cue!'

The vines all tangled, seek the sun,
'Let's play hide and seek, oh what fun!'
Petals flit like butterflies,
In this lush world, laughter flies.

So if you stroll through blooms so bright,
Listen close, delight in their flight.
For flora's tales, both wild and free,
Are filled with jokes, just wait and see!

The Garden's Lullaby

At dusk, the garden sings a tune,
To crickets under the silver moon.
Petunias sway while tulips yawn,
'Was that a cat or the grass' own fawn?'

Mice in hats join the serenade,
They've formed a band, a grand brigade.
With acorn drums and berry flutes,
Every night, they dress in roots.

The roses snicker, 'What are they doing?'
As the lavender laughs, the fun still brewing.
But watch for the frog on the lily pad,
His terrible tunes will make you mad!

So come and bask in nature's jest,
With every plant, a merry fest.
In this orchestra of green delight,
The laughter echoes, sweet and light.

A Tapestry of Colors

Reds and yellows, colors tease,
A canvas spread in the gentle breeze.
The marigold trips, spills its hue,
Laughing at violets, claiming it too!

Green stays quiet, but oh, so sly,
Creeping under the roses' eye.
'You'll never guess the shade I'm wearing,'
'It's called envy, while you're all blaring!'

The backdrop whispers jokes untold,
Leaves tumble lightly, brave and bold.
With nature's brush, a riot painted,
In every shade, the garden's tainted.

So lift your spirit with colors bright,
Where flowers jest, and hues take flight.
In this tapestry of blooms divine,
Every petal's laughter, intertwined.

Through Petals and Time

In a charming nook, the blossoms dance,
Every flower dressed, ready to prance.
Daisies waltz under careful stars,
While daisies munch on cute candy bars.

The wind tells tales of pollen's flight,
Of butterflies causing quite a fright.
'Oh dear!' the lilacs gasp in fright,
'That butterfly looks close to a kite!'

The petals chuckle at sun's warm coax,
As bumblebees perform wild hoaxes.
They spin around, their buzz a hum,
But beware when the ants start to drum!

So join the fun, let laughter sprout,
In petals' grip, we twist and shout.
Through the blooms of joy and cheer,
A garden's dream, forever near!

The Allure of Verdant Trails

In the garden, a snail took a stroll,
Wearing a hat that was just a bit small.
He said with a grin, 'I'm on a grand quest!'
But really, he just needed a place to rest.

The flowers all giggled, their petals a-flutter,
As the snail ventured forth, what a curious utter!
He slipped on a leaf, went sailing like a boat,
Landing right next to an old, wise toad.

'What brings you here, in your shell so round?'
The toad chuckled lightly, his voice sweet and sound.
'Just looking for laughs and a friend to share,
The secrets of life or the best garden fare.'

With blooms and with grins, they danced in the sun,
Plotting their mischief and how to have fun.
For who knew that snail could have such a tale,
In the allure of the paths where the wild ones prevail!

Dance of the Wildflowers

In a meadow where daisies wore sun hats so bright,
A poppy exclaimed, 'Let's dance through the night!'
The daisies agreed, with a sway and a clap,
Creating a rhythm, then sharing a nap.

Butterflies flitted, making quite the fuss,
While a clumsy old bee caused a great deal of bus.
'Excuse me,' he buzzed, 'Is this spot mine or yours?'
The daisies just giggled, 'Make room for our floors!'

With petals all twirling and colors so bold,
They laughed at the bee, who was stuck in a fold.
'Join us,' they beckoned, 'In this waltz of the day,
We'll tickle the sun with our petals at play!'

So they twirled and they spun, like a playful parade,
In a humorous dance that the flowers had made.
And the magic of mischief, in blooms filled with cheer,
Turned a simple old meadow to a ballroom sincere!

A Floral Retrospective

Oh, the roses recalled their youthful days,
When they pranced in the breeze, a delightful ballet.
Their fragrance was charming, they blushed with pure glee,
Now they reminisce in this elderberry tree.

The tulips all chuckled, their colors so bright,
'We once had a crush on a shy daffodil knight!'
But alas, he was taken by a cheeky old fern,
Thus ending their hopes with a twist at each turn.

The violets chimed in with their sweet little woes,
'We tried to impress, but our perfume just froze!'
They laughed 'til they cried at the tales of delight,
While planning their pranks for the next springtime night.

Each flower recalled, with petals ablaze,
A myriad of moments, a colorful maze.
In the garden of laughter, the past is a cheer,
For blooms with a wink make each memory dear!

Nature's Quiet Murmurs

In the hush of the woods, a squirrel had dreams,
Of acorns and mischief, or so it seems.
With a twitch of his tail and a dash through the leaves,
He plotted the craziest of heists on the eaves!

The rabbits all chuckled, their ears standing tall,
As the squirrel scampered, he'd surely take a fall.
'Watch out for the birds!' a wise owl did hoot,
'Or you'll end up in trouble, when seeking your loot!'

With stealthy finesse, he approached the prize,
A stash of sweet nuts, oh what a surprise!
But just as he grabbed, the branch gave a crack,
And down came a shower of leaves on his back.

Yet still, he just laughed, with a light-hearted spin,
For even in folly, he knew he would win.
In nature's soft laughter, the whispers revealed,
The joy of the chase is the treasure concealed!

The Dancing Bloom

In the garden, a flower plays,
Bobbing its head in sunny rays.
With petals twirling, it takes a chance,
Inviting bees to join the dance.

It spins and hops on the breeze,
Chasing butterflies, if you please.
A wink and giggle at the sky,
Flower's the star, oh my, oh my!

The dew drops glisten, the ants applaud,
While the sun smiles down, not even flawed.
What a silly sight indeed,
Nature's jesters, in flowery speed!

So gather round for the blooming show,
Marvel at the fun, let laughter flow.
In petals and stamen, joy is found,
The dancing bloom spins 'round and 'round!

Secrets in Scented Shadows

Whispers from petals, secrets unfold,
A fragrance so sweet, never gets old.
Roses gossip with daisies bright,
Sharing stories in the soft moonlight.

Tulips chuckle, their blooms in a row,
Planning a party, don't tell the snow!
They wear their colors, vibrant and bold,
While marigolds tease with tales untold.

In the dark, a garden so sly,
Hidden jokes make the night fly by.
Lilies murmur, a whimsical chant,
Conspiring with daisies to pull a prank.

Tiptoeing creatures, laughs in the dew,
Buds sneaking giggles, who knew?
Under the cover of leaves and of dark,
Scented shadows leave their mark!

Wandering Through Floral Dreams

A wanderer steps through blooms of delight,
With petals painting the path in light.
Each fragrance pulls, 'Come join the spree!'
A lilac whispers, 'Don't you see?'

Sunflowers tower, they guard the way,
With a nod and wink, they beg one to stay.
While violets prank with their sweet little charms,
To lure the lost into nature's arms.

In a daisy meadow, giggles abound,
As bees make stories without a sound.
A breeze brings laughter, oh what a scene,
As flowers conspire like a well-practiced team!

Wandering in dreams, with colors that twirl,
Nature's circus, a whimsical whirl.
In floral whispers, the heart takes flight,
Every petal's a promise, pure delight!

A Traveler's Embrace

A traveler arrives with a smile so wide,
Hugging the blooms, wishing to bide.
With every glance, a tale to exchange,
Petals welcome in the sweetest range.

Morning glories yawn, stretching in glee,
Inviting the traveler to sip on tea.
With butterflies fluttering, laughter in tow,
Together they venture where nobody knows.

Tulips and poppies play tag in the field,
While the breeze tells secrets, unsealed.
"Oh, what a journey! What adventures await?"
The traveler chuckles, "Oh, isn't this great?"

With a fragrant embrace, they share a toast,
To blossoms and giggles, they cherish the most.
So come, take a step, let your worries erase,
For in nature's arms lies a warm, bright embrace!

Whispers of a Floral Odyssey

In a garden, flowers meet,
They giggle, oh so sweet.
Daisy whispers, bluebell beams,
Saying, "Plan a party, or so it seems!"

The roses rolled their eyes, so plush,
While sunflowers danced in a rush.
Bumblebees buzzed with flair,
"Who brought the snacks!" gave them a scare!

Tulips tangoed, lilies twirled,
A floral fest, their joy unfurled.
Petunias snickered, their leaves in curls,
"Watch out, here comes that bee who swirls!"

A sunflower slipped, and what a sight,
The petals flew, oh what delight!
With laughter ringing through the air,
Floral friendships without a care.

Auroras of Aroma

In dawn's embrace, scents collide,
Like a wild ride on a floral slide.
Lavender laughs with a hint of sass,
"Who knew today would turn to grass?"

Mint chimed in, all spruced and bright,
"Let's brew some tea, what a delight!"
But daisies cried, in a fit of glee,
"Who's steeping tea? This is a spree!"

Carnations pranced, aware of the game,
Competing for names, not one was the same.
"Call me cute, call me fair,
Just don't forget my fragrant flair!"

As marigolds twirled and violets spun,
They claimed that their blooms were second to none.
In a riot of colors, they spun and they swayed,
Aroma auroras, all laughter displayed!

The Secret Life of Petals

Have you heard the gossip of petals' play?
At twilight's dance, they scurry away.
With whispers of nectar, secrets unfold,
Under the moon, stories retold.

Rosettes argue about who's the best,
"Just look at my hues, I'm clearly blessed!"
While daisies claim with a cheeky grin,
"I'm the star! Let the dance begin!"

Tulips try yoga, stretching their stems,
While orchids tease with their fancy hems.
But lavender snoozes, blissfully unaware,
In the leafy cover, she's out without care.

As petals chuckle through the soft breeze,
They share wild dreams of the sweetest tease.
In gardens at night, their laughs intertwine,
A whimsical secret, simply divine!

In Search of Garden Wonders

A quest for blooms, oh what a thrill,
"Who's the funniest flower?" they giggle and shrill.
The lilies were sure they'd take the crown,
While petunias said, "Come on, calm down!"

They hunted for laughs in a leafy maze,
With daffodils singing in sunny rays.
Hummingbirds joined, with buzz and with cheer,
"Each bloom has a joke, lend us your ear!"

From the vibrant violets to roses' own flair,
Every petal shared tales without a care.
"Why did the flower refuse to bloom?
It couldn't find space, it felt like a room!"

In search of joy, they danced through the sun,
In the heart of the garden, they all had fun.
With petals a-twirl and laughter anew,
In every flower, a miracle grew!

Secrets Among the Green

In a garden where whispers play,
A snail told secrets, oh what a day!
The roses giggled, petals aflutter,
While the worms chuckled, deep in the utter.

The daisies danced, a burst of cheer,
Who knew plants could hold such dear?
An ant wore a hat and strutted around,
Claiming he'd find the best picnic ground.

A cabbage rolled dice, quite a surprise,
With lettuce nearby, counting the pies!
The carrots told jokes, oh what a thrill,
While the thyme just sighed, "Let's climb this hill!"

So in this green realm, laughter was king,
With each leafy character, joy would spring!
In the garden of jokes, no need for a ruler,
Just a happy leaf knows, life's much cooler!

Journey to the Heart of Bloom

A bumblebee buzzed with a quirky grin,
He brought his hat, oh what a win!
He met a flower with a voice so bold,
"Buzz on, dear friend, let's break the mold!"

Together they traveled through colors so bright,
Sipping on nectar, oh what a delight!
A butterfly joked, "What's the buzz about?"
As petals entwined, they danced all about.

The tulips in a chorus sang silly tunes,
Under the gaze of a plump round moon.
They tickled the daisies with petals so fine,
And laughed at the thorns who couldn't join the line.

At the heart of bloom, joy overflowed,
Where laughter sprouted and friendship glowed.
In this garden fun, worries took flight,
Forever in bloom, beneath the starlight!

A Palette of Petal Dreams

In a whimsical world of colors and schemes,
Petals painted joy with hilarious dreams.
A red rose joked with a yellow and blue,
"Let's mix it up, yes, a rainbow crew!"

They splashed through puddles of dew with glee,
While pansies pulled pranks, oh can't you see?
A violet snickered, a real funny sight,
As the clouds chuckled, trying to stay light.

"Hey there, daisies, what's your best plan?"
Said a bold petunia by a tiny can.
With a wink of a stalk, the group made a club,
Where everything flourished, not a single drub!

So they danced 'round the garden in a playful mess,
Creating a canvas of joy—nothing less!
In the palette of petal dreams they spun,
Painting laughter and love, a whole new fun!

Routes of the Fruitful Wanderer

A wanderer wandered with snacks in tow,
On a journey of fruit, oh wouldn't you know?
With lemons for hats and berries for shoes,
He chuckled at nature's colorful views!

He met an apple who cracked a sly joke,
"Watch out for bananas, they slip when they poke!"
Grapes joined the fun, in clusters they swayed,
While cherries giggled, their confidence displayed.

Through orchards they traipsed, singing sweet songs,
Chasing a wind that was playfully strong.
A peach offered hugs, wrapped in its fluff,
Saying "Life's a treat, let's munch on this stuff!"

So on went the wanderer, the fruity team,
Creating a bubble of laughter and dream.
In the route of the fruitful, all was never grey,
With every step taken, they brightened the way!

Pathways of Aromatic Travel

In a garden of scents, I walk with glee,
Daisies tease me, 'Come dance, you'll see!'
Sniffing each flower, I hop and I skip,
Oh, what a riot, plant party, no trip!

Petals giggle as butterflies zoom,
They whisper, 'Join us, we need some room!'
A bee buzzes in asking for a spare,
'Why so serious? Just cut loose, do care!'

Each fragrance a ticket, I slip on a shoe,
Stumbling on blooms, now I'm joined by a crew.
We laugh at the weeds, they're just misconstrued,
When you're twirling with flowers, you can't be rude!

So off we all wander, a floral parade,
Of laughter and petals, no plans to invade.
Just fragrant delight with every step I take,
In this silly garden, there's fun to make!

Harmony in Blossom

In the meadow, a trumpet flower plays,
Teasing the daisies in sun's warm rays.
Hummingbirds giggle, sipping sweet dew,
While the roses blush, oh, what a view!

Petunias crowd around, cracking a joke,
'What did the tulip say? I'm no oak!'
Laughter erupts from stalks waving high,
What fun to be leafy, oh my, oh my!

A sunflower winks, with seeds all aglow,
'These petals are armed, but we won't throw!'
With vines that entwine like old friends at play,
The garden's a stage, and humor holds sway!

As I wander, I chuckle at every turn,
With each floral smile, laughter I earn.
It's a festival, nature's quirky charade,
A fragrant delight that'll never fade!

The Winding Floral Path

Down the winding path, I stumble and swerve,
Where tangle of blossoms takes all of my verve.
A daffodil called for a game of charades,
While violets snickered, 'Where's your crusade?'

Chasing a comet of dandelion fluff,
I tripped on a crocus, oh, that's quite tough!
With petals in tangles, and laughter in stride,
Nature's a playground, where giggles reside!

Rosemary rolled, with thyme at her heels,
On this floral freeway, justice appeals.
Pansies throw shade in the best playful way,
Together they spin tales that brighten the day!

So I breathe in the fun with each fragrant turn,
In this flowery comedy, there's much to learn.
As I navigate with joy in my heart,
Every giggle and chuckle is nature's fine art!

The Pursuit of Petal Serenity

Amidst a garden's quirky embrace,
Each petal a puzzle, each stem has a place.
I chase a rose, hoping to find some peace,
But the daisies humor, saying, 'Never cease!'

With blossoms that giggle, I trip on a vine,
'Keep up with us, dear, don't fall out of line!'
Lavenders whisper, spreading sweet cheer,
They know that the best blooms are funny and dear.

As I stumble through fragrance, laughter takes flight,
With campy tall tales that reach dizzying height.
Each flower a jester with petals at play,
In this pursuit of happiness, I dance all day!

So when seeking peace, just be ready to roam,
In a garden of giggles, you'll feel right at home.
For petals will whisper, with charm so sincere,
Embrace the rich humor that blooms every year!

Where Aromas Paint the Sky

In fields of scents, we dance and play,
With nose in the air, we chase the sway.
A bee buzzes past, asks for a sip,
"Did you forget? I'm busy with this trip!"

Lemonade clouds and minty airstream,
We stumble and giggle, lost in a dream.
The flowers gossip in whispers and sighs,
As we twirl and tumble beneath their guise.

A breeze brings laughter, it tickles our toes,
Roses compete with the scent of my nose.
We stick candy flowers in our sun hat,
While bugs run a marathon, it's time for a chat!

With petals like paper, we write our own fate,
The aroma of chaos, it's never too late.
In gardens of giggles, we conquer the hours,
Where aromas paint joy in wayward flowers.

Blooming Echoes of an Aged Garden

In an old garden where memories bloom,
The plants wear glasses to fight off the gloom.
A wise old daisy teaches tales of the night,
While the roses just blush, shining so bright.

"What's the secret to your endless cheer?"
The geranium replies, "Just add some beer!"
With roots intertwined, they laugh 'til they cry,
While the sunflowers dance as the clouds pass by.

Gnome statues chuckle at our clumsy prance,
As we trip on the daisies, caught in a trance.
The moon peeks out with a wink in the sky,
While the lettuce gossips, "Oh my, oh my!"

With honeycombed laughter, the garden's a stage,
Where flowers swap stories and antics engage.
An aged crew blooming with humor each day,
In echoes of laughter, we'll always stay.

The Fragrance of Forgotten Tales

In a cupboard of scents, where stories lie,
An old lemon chunk winks, it's ready to fly.
With each whisk of vanilla, a giggle is spun,
While cinnamon bakes tales of mischief and fun.

A mint leaf recounts how it danced on the breeze,
As garlic just sighs, "I'm too strong for these."
While peppercorn laughs at the old cheese with pride,
"Oh, to be young again when I took that ride!"

Baking fills hearts with a warm, tender glow,
While a rogue chili whispers, "Let's put on a show!"
Forgotten could be where whimsy resides,
In blends of old spices, where laughter abides.

In jars of nostalgia, we stir in delight,
Where each whiff of past brings a chuckle at night.
Concocting sweet chaos, we lift up our tails,
As we dive into flavors and forgotten tales.

Beneath the Canopy of Stars

Under the stars with a prankster moon,
We jest with the crickets in a silly tune.
The fireflies blink with a cheeky stare,
While the grasshoppers leap without a care.

A dog named Fido leads the parade,
In a cloak made of leaves, he's the ultimate grade!
We throw popcorn at the plump, puffy clouds,
While giggles erupt among the wild crowds.

With a blanket of laughter, we gaze at the night,
The cosmos chuckling, shining so bright.
Stars sprinkle stories as we lay and dream,
Crafting our future like a whimsical stream.

Underneath these wonders, where fun never pales,
The night whispers secrets, life's vast holy grails.
In the canopy of starlight, let your heart soar,
Where joy is the compass, and laughter's the door!

www.ingramcontent.com/pod-product-compliance
Lightning Source LLC
Chambersburg PA
CBHW071821160426
43209CB00003B/154

9781805667247